Copyright 2009 By Keisha Watson
ISBN: 978-0-578-03219-1

PAIN

Table of Contents

Dedicated to "T"	3,4
Why I Write	5
Being Mentally Abused	6
The Way I Am	7
If I die Today	8
Why Do I cry	9
So Weak	10
LIFE	12
Lucky	13
I lost	14
I'll Choose for You	15
I Remember	16
When you're in love	17
Rest In Peace	18
I love you for you	20
Sometimes	21
You Love Me and You Care?	22
That Overdose	23
Without thinking Twice	24
Shades of Blue	25
The Game	27
All Around I'm Faithful	28

Hurt People, Hurt People	29
A Woman's Body	30
You hurt Me	31
Only You Understand You	32
I Want You for You	33
Where is this going	34
Just Rain On Me	36
Why Me God	37
Thank You	38

Dedicated to "T"

Dedicated to "T" that encouraged me to go forth and write poetry.
Dedicated to "T" that has never disowned or banded me.
For being my earthly father sent from our father above,
For always telling me to keep my head up, and who encouraged me to love.
For being the first person that showed unconditional love to me,
And for being that close friend I thought there could never be.
For correcting me when I was wrong and for encouraging me to keep going
For teaching me the games they play on the streets,
And just for allowing me to be me.
For teaching me that I wasn't the floor and not to let people walk over me,
For standing up for me and showing me things I'd thought I never see.
Just for being so strong and able and willing to handle me.
For taking time just to show you care,
For going out your way just to be there.
For arguing with me, even know you know you'll never win,
For real, just being my best friend.
For being the arms God blessed me with to protect me at night,
I know your not perfect, but when it comes to me your alright.
For allowing me to smile and frown,
And most of all, teaching me to turn around.
Turn around from wrong and even sometimes right
Turn around and see what's on the other side
Turn around and explore and see,
Most of all turn around and be happy.
For telling me struggle is good,
And teaching me everything's not always like it should.
It has to be hard to get easy,
And through that journey he'll hold me.
For feeding, and clothing me when I couldn't do it myself,
Just for been my right hand when I needed help.

For always putting me first in whatever needed to be done,
And for encouraging me whatever I do, I've already won.
For assisting me with those extra steps I really needed help in,
For allowing me to open my heart and love again
For saving my life when I thought I couldn't make it anymore,
For being that friend that held secrets and gave me the key to the door.
Just for making sure I was all right before anyone else in his life,
For giving me his last without thinking twice.
For allowing me to live my life and be free,
And for the few years of nothing but encouraging me.
And for allowing me to try the three most difficult things i have problems saying,

    I love you,

    I need help and

    I'm sorry

Dedicated to "T" who has been there for me since day one of my poetry book and haven't left yet,
Dedicated to "T" that will be in my life always, with no regrets.
Dedicated to "T" who I love with all of me heart,
Dedicated to "T" that the bond and friendship we have will never tear apart.
Pain wrong turn is dedicated to "T". That God sent to me so that I could grow a little bit stronger with and learn to express myself.
This book is dedicated to TyJuan Hodge who I love and trust with all of my heart.
One Heart!
One Love!
One Way In!
NO Way Out!
Love Yourself First And Always!!!

Why I Write

I write when I feel good and I write when I feel bad

I even write when I'm angry and mad

A pin creates wonderful things and allows me to express my thoughts and feelings

And the paper is where I write everything down and then I begin to see God's healings

It encourages me to live life until the end

Writing is truly my best friend it teaches me that I am able to do whatever I want to do

And it also teaches me that all of my dreams are able to come true

A way to express myself and a way to let out steam

My way of saying whatever I want, nice or mean

When I write I feel free

And my writing is how I express me

I love to write and I love to read

It's like my garden and I'm planting every seed

I write because it's me

And most of all I write because this is something that keeps me smiling and happy

BEING MENTALLY ABUSED

You can't imagine how hard it is finding someone who cares

Looking for a love one to talk to when you're scared

Beings abused mentally and told that your ugly and no one will ever like you

These are some of the things people say and do

Being mentally misused by all the people who claim they care and love you

Forced to be blind so your eyes can't see

They talk about you behind your back and smile in your face

Then want to right and tell you when your out of place

Feeling weird because your family disown you the most

Then when you need them they disappear like ghosts

Out of all the people you expect them to be there

The people you don't expect are the real ones who care

Being mentally abused has forced me to build a lock to my heart

Having so called friends and family tear it apart

I'm just trying to find the one person I can trust and love

The Way I Am

Many people ask, why am I the way I am?

How is it possible that I could do something stupid over a man

It's just not the man it's the person I've grown to be

This person that thought she had built love and trust and for the first time was happy

This person that cried herself to sleep every night

Then this man came alone understood her and held her tight

Many people ask, why do I do what I do?

In situations when the shoe is on the other foot, what about you?

I was this strong black young lady that had dreams just like every one else

But continually friends and family made me feel by myself

I never wanted to feel isolated and have a whole in my heart

These are my stories of how people just force me to tear myself apart

And no, not just men, friends and most of all my family

I always felt because I was different they didn't care for me

I have my own path and vision of life, and I guess that's what got me where I am

I'm this poor little girl that's in love with a man

If I Die Today

If I die today I sleep through tomorrow
And if I die today you'll know for a fact my life ended in sorrow
Sorrow and pain because you and I both know we played the game
Slapped in the face by Carmen itself
And left to fend for nobody but yourself
Cry yourself to sleep every night and hurt yourself every hour
You felt so weak you've lost your power
The power that allowed you to control your every movement
And that power that allowed you to erase every moment spent
Or maybe I'll just give it one more day
So I'll have one more chance to get it right while I bow my head and pray
I'll pray that God will take my soul and protect me while I lay
And speak through me so I'll have nothing but good things to say
You taught me as much as I taught you
And you gave me so much more than I gave you
And to throw it all away is the easy way out and the only way we know
We get angry and sometimes it's hard to let our true feeling show
We may call each other out of our names and show we don't care
But when it comes down to the truth you and I both know what's there
And what's there is you and I
You and I left to stand, or left to fall

Why Do I Cry

Why do I cry?
Why don't I cry should be the question
I cry to release the pain
And I cry when people think my life is just a game
I look in the mirror as tears run down my face
The tears come out so fast I think my eyes are having a race
Why do I cry?
I feel alone
When you look at me you don't know what's going on
You don't understand what I've been through
Many say smile
But how can I smile when I forgot how
How can I be happy?
When I see it's not for me
Why do I live everyday wishing it was my last
And why do I feel like I'm living in the past
Why do I cry?
Look at my life
I thought long and hard about taking it, but I had to think twice
I hold in so much and I have no one to talk to
So when I'm alone here's something that I do
I cry
    I hurt
        I cry
            I feel
                I cry
                    I'm alone
                        I cry
                            I'm scared
                        I cry
                  I cry
            I cry

STILL WHY?

SO WEAK

I want to let go but it seems like I cant
Because you and I became one and if I let go of you I'll be letting go of myself
It's getting harder and harder as each day passes by
And I'm so insecure because all I do is cry
I cry because I'm scared and afraid of being alone
I try everyday to make you happy and stay out of your way
And it seems like all I'm doing is pushing you further and further away
I know I love you and want to be with you
But sometimes I feel like what we have been done and threw
We taught each other what we needed to grow
And it's been time that we let each other go
I feel like I'm hanging onto you so tight, I let go of myself
Because at this point I put more into making you happy than myself
I strive everyday to make sure you're all right
And I'm the one who really needs help
Because I lost my self-esteem right alone with everything else
I pretend I'm happy and that my life is okay
I've even became so weak I hold my tongue when I have something to say
I put you first in my life, heart and everything I do
I just have one question; Do you do the same thing to?
Because if you did it wouldn't be so easy for you to go days without speaking to me
And you would probably want to spend more than one or two hours with me
I've became so weak I don't eat
So weak all I do is cry myself to sleep
So weak I don't allow myself to think
So weak because I allowed you to sweep me off my feet.

You are the author of your life,
Just keep in mind you're writing in pen,
And can not erase your doings!!

LIFE

What would the world be without nothing

Lost people and souls looking for something

A tear worth to cry for

And in that same scene worth to die for

People wanting everything you've got

And really what you're living for isn't a lot

Free space, free air

The good life blinded by a glare

And not in the sky

Instead the weakened eye

What you need is indeed in sight

But were so unsure maybe it doesn't feel right

But in life we always choose the other side

Because when times get ruff our eyes cant find a place to hide

Lucky

Here I am
Beautiful I am
This girl, this girl,
  Could have any man
Lucky you, she choose you
Choose you to be with her and do all you can do
This girl so fine and smart,
Knew you would some day come alone and play with her heart
But the object of the game was not to fall in
Into the feeling of one day sayin'
  Damn, deep down inside, I love this man
Now Lucky me, I feel into a shape
A shape that has so much meaning, I hate
Three corners waiting for a name
And three corners that weren't aware of the shame
To say I'm dieing from a deadly disease, is a lie
So can I tell you the reason why eyes cry
Who cares, Love or hate
But don't ever go a day and not tell me what you don't appreciate

I Lost

How is it possible that I lost when you never gave me the chance to win?
And you never brung it to my attention that your past has no end
It's so hard to smile when you see your life walking away
And you want to fall to your knees but you don't know what to say
It feels good to have that one person make your life feel complete and whole
Even better when that person becomes your heart and soul
But what's left to live for when you begin to drift apart
Because everything is worth to die for when you have a broken heart
You couldn't imagine the pain I feel
Because I thought I found love and I thought it was real
I thought forever you and I would be
And I thought finally after 20 years I'll be happy
I'm not to young to know what love feels like
And I'm not too stupid to know when some things not right
I'm so scared to ever love again
And I cant live knowing were just friends
I think I was just here to help you grow
So go on and grow and let me go
I'm giving up because it's no way I'm going to win
And I love you so much, but I don't think I could ever be with you again

I'll choose for you

I feel so confused because I asked a simple question and that was to choose
Her or me who do you want to be with
Because you and I know it's me that's every moment spent with
You say you don't care but I know the real feelings that are there
But when she comes around you refuse to let them show
And that made me feel like my time was up and I had to go
When she's around you always seem to look past me and when she's not around it's all about me
I want to be with you and it seems you do to
But you also want both of us and I'm sorry because I can't allow that wish to come true
You say you love me and want to be with me but the pain I feel from you I feel like it's just a game
I'll always be your friend and I thought we'd be together until the end
But you allowed your so-called ex to make me feel like I can't trust you again
Love has its many different rules, but I've learned it's up to you to choose
Choose which one's you'll allow yourself to be happy with
And which one's you allow to spend your every moment with
Maybe I'm not forever material because you can't allow your heart to shift
Shift from one love to a greater and let go of the past
And the in creditable feelings you and I share will last
But now it's up to you, because I already choose you
You should leave your baggage behind
Because by you continuing to hang on to it and knowing someday I might find
You can show you care or don't, but either way I'll end up hurt
So while you stand in the middle and choose who you want
I'll stop being stupid and make it easier for you by letting go
Now you don't have to choose anymo'

I Remember

That smile like I us to smile
That butterfly feeling that I had when you came around
How my heart would beat crazy when I heard your voice
How when I was with you , I felt safe and sound
I use to turn around and by my surprise see your face
That good morning phone call to start my day
The little text messages that made me feel good
The way you spent your time and money with me
Then that day you said, I love you, my feelings changed
The want and drive I had for you became stronger
That kiss on my forehead, covered my body in chills
I knew from the first day we went out my feelings were real
Now I love you so much I don't want to let you go
I'm happy everyday even if it doesn't show
I love when we make up from a fight or argument
Most of all I love every moment spent

When You're In Love

When you're in love that's the only person you'll see
You want be attracted to anyone else or even fill confused
If your ashamed or embarrassed to say or show you love
      Then you don't really love
Care and love are two different things
Two different feelings and two different levels of dedication
When you're in love all of the feelings will be there and you'll know their real
You'll naturally put that person first in everything you do
When you're in love no questions will have to be asked
Because all of your feelings will do the talking
You'll began to feel a one on one connection
And you'll began to feel the love that's meant for you
One touch will give you chills and cover your body with grace
Another touch just might make you feel complete and whole
When you're in love trust yourself because you'll know
You might find yourself doing things differently and smiling a little bit more
The presence of that person you'll share will be the best part of the day
By scent or sight that's the only person you'll find from a distance
You'll build love so strong and hard that no one will tear it apart
At least no one you allow to enter your heart
That's when you're in love.

Rest In Peace

If I don't make it to see tomorrow
You'll have love on the other side and for me you'll feel no sorrow

Because your happiness is going to last until you say it's the end
My happiness isn't going to last because I'll meet no one like you again

You gave me your all, but yet, I don't have your all

I'm in love with you because you're the only one my heart sees
You're the only one that I want to be with
You're the only one that makes me cry
And you're the only one that cares about me

That's love good and bad
That's love to carry me along when I'm sad

Love has it's own package and comes in many different ways
It seems like our love is like the ocean because it has so many different tides and waves

If I don't make it to see will you miss me
Because I can't allow you to hurt me
And I can't allow me to hurt me

I cut my risks to calm down
And I cut my risks to erase the frown

I can't do it anymore and I want out
Because it seems like no one hears me when I shout

I feel alone and by myself
And when I finish writing this there'll be no one else

Because at this point I don't know what to do
Don't know who is who

Because all I have is you , and without you I don't want it to be a me
So I'll take my life and wish me the best that I'll Rest In Peace

LOVE YOURSELF FIRST AND ALWAYS!

I want you for you

I was down for you
And there for everything we've been through
You taught me
And I taught you
We shared laughs and memories I hope you never forget
Even told each other all our secrets
We shared all our deepest fears
Everything we wanted in a person was there
Funny because we slowly grew apart
And I actually felt you slipping from my heart
Your touch had started to change and the way you looked at me
And from you feeling a certain way, I felt an certain way, and became unhappy
I can sit and tell you everything I want in a man
But then you'll act on everything, and that means you really don't understand
When I tell you what I want in a man, doesn't mean for you to change
It simply means to rearrange
Don't change the person you are, to become someone your not
That simply means, work with what you've got
I don't know who you're trying to be
But I do know you once was that person who truly made me happy

Sometimes

Sometimes I close my eyes and I can see your face looking at me
Then sometimes it hurts my brain thinking and wondering were you might be

And even sometimes I find it hard to sleep at night because your on my mind
Sometimes I just want you to call and say, "hey baby, I'm doing fine"

Sometimes I wonder are you really happy being with me
Then sometimes I've wondered why do I pretend like everything is okay and your not hurting me

Then I want to know are you really in love with me
Then sometimes I want to know why is your heart locked and who has the key

Sometimes I feel like I've lost my best friend
Then sometimes I feel like whatever it is we have has to end

Sometimes I want to know as I someone you can see yourself with forever
Because at times I wonder are we really meant to be together

Sometimes I think maybe you found someone else
And even sometimes I feel like you dust me off to do something else

And sometimes I get angry because I feel like your not giving me your all
So sometimes I wonder who's occupying your time when you don't call

Sometimes I feel like I'm going to loose you and never see you again
Then sometimes I feel like were just friends

Sometimes I want to ask you some of these things
But every time I try to ask you some of these things it seems your business and the telephone just rings.

You Love Me And You Care?

So you say you love me and you say you care
And throughout everything you'll promise to be there

You promised to be my friend and ride out to the end
Through good or bad, thick or thin, *three* years ago, my life began

You turned my frowns into smiles
Took me the extra miles

You taught me things I never knew
And many thanks to you, because I've learned and grew

We created a bond so tight and so strong
That no matter what happens we'll be together right or wrong

The hardiest thing in life is letting go
And trying to hide your emotions and feelings and not let them show

But what do you do when you made the biggest mistake on your life
Because if you could go back and rewind time, you would without thinking twice

Throughout the process you've lost yourself
And without knowing you pointed the finger at someone else

You hurt deep down inside
But no one knows because you cover it up and hide

So why do I look around everyday and find myself alone
And when I look in the mirror I see apart of me gone

But you said you loved me and you said you cared
And you said throughout everything you promised to be there

That Overdose

Its hard growing up and being torn apart from your family
And been pushed to the side and told you don't understand, as if you can't see

Having mama strung out on drugs and telling you everything is going to be okay
With no food to eat, alone sitting in the dark, and all you can do is pray

Pray to God and hope he can hear you pass all the crying and pain
And hope when you open your eyes nothing will be the same

Because mama sick in the head
And grandma sick in the bed

And your siblings are all you have, but still they don't understand
Instead of mama taking care of her kids and household she runs out with some man

This man that has forced her not to love her kids and support them
This man that she allowed to rape her daughter, and told her she needed it and it would never happen again

That crack, that high that only last a few hours, is tearing your kids life apart
Because their growing up without love in their mother's heart

Shortly but soon after that she dies of an overdose
That overdose that caused her kids to grow up without a mother
That overdose that caused her kids to split up
That overdose that she needed and wanted so bad
That overdose that left her kids feeling even more alone and sad

WITHOUT THINKING TWICE

Always striving and giving my all
Putting others first and end up filling like my back is against the wall

Feeling like I'm not good enough to keep our love strong
I'm so faithful to you and I promise I don't do anything wrong

I put you first in my life and my heart
And the love I have for you I will never let anyone tear it apart

Trapped with my back against the wall and afraid to walk straight
Because I know I gave my all and it seems like he doesn't appreciate

Appreciate the fact that I love him so much and give him my all
But it seems like my life has been wasted and I'm going to fall

Fall in my grave and maybe take my life
Because how I feel right now I don't want to think twice

To die will release the pain
and to die is the reward we get after falling in love with the game

I feel ashamed and alone because the person I've fail in love with seems gone
Seems gone and out my life because I'm dieing without thinking twice

Stressed and not the same me
I need help but to turn and ask is the mirror and I only see me

Standing alone with my life in my hand and taking it away
Slowly but surely I'll crumble it and watch myself die with nothing left to say

Shades of blue

It's shades of blue

That you keep putting me through

Got me up and down

I smile and then I frown

It seems like the sky is falling down

Since you haven't been around

And when you are I still feel the same way

Because how can I trust, when I don't believe a word you say

And how can I love when I'm heading the wrong way

And why should I pray, when I bow my head and have nothing to say

Shades of blue, is suppose to be part of the phases of love

But, What do you do when you're the only one in love?

WHEN THINGS SEEM IMPOSSIBLE PRAY!

That Game

I was by your side through the good and the bad
I was the one who allowed you to express yourself when you were mad

I gave you my heart and I gave you my soul
And after all the nights you beat me I never let go

I waited on you hand and foot for seven good years
And for six years I seen myself in tears

Tears that didn't even express my true pain
Because I've been married to you and you been married to the game

That game that controlled you and told you it was okay to cheat
That game that encouraged you and told you it was okay to beat

That game that allowed you to hear your children scream and cry
That game that forced you to lie

That game has completely tore us apart
And at this very moment I don't feel love in my heart

I gave you my life and soul
But now it's time I do something for me and let you go

All Around I'm Faithful

I'm faithful with my heart because you're the only one who has a key
And I'm faithful with my ears, because I can hear you footsteps if I were blind and couldn't see
And with my smile because it's filled with happiness that only you can bring

I'm faithful with my mouth because every time I speak it's of you
And I'm faithful with my arms because you're the only one I engrace with a hug
And my lips because you're the only one I'll leave with a kiss

I'm faithful with my feet because you where my heart allows me to walk
And I'm faithful with my eyes because in a group you're the only one I would see
And with my nose because I can sense you in a crowd

I'm faithful with my mind because all I do is think about you
And I'm faithful with my body because you're the only one I'll ever allow to touch
And with my pin, because you're the only one I'll send poems and love notes to

I'm faithful with my spirit because without you who will keep me alive
Because I just might die

Hurt People, Hurt People

You're sad and your hurt, so you talk about me
You know how it feels to be hurt so it's easy for you to hurt me
You've been disrespected and maybe even felt alone
So you spread rumors, and thought my friends would be gone
You treat me as if I'm trash and different from you
You don't like me and you want everyone to feel like that to
Hurt People, Hurt People

Have you been lied on, cheated on, mistreated and not wanted
Or have you been called ugly, stupid, dumb, and told you'll never be anything
Or have you even been told you're a hoe, tramp, or even what they call a female dog
Have you been called a bastard, trick, fat, retarded and slow
Or have you been called big forehead, bold head, foster child
Or maybe you've been called dirty and been told you'll never be good for anything or even been told, I wish you die
I Have

Hurt people, hurt people
Not all hurt people hurt people, I've been hurt and its not a good feeling
So why do you think hurt people, hurt people?
They hurt because they hurt
They haven't allowed their body to heal from the hurt and the pain so its still there and growing
So their mind and heart is focused on hurting others because they still hurt themselves
Some hurt people, hurt people, but not all hurt people, hurt people
Am I a person that hurts people?

A Woman's Body

Built strong and firm, made to smile

Built with a strong heart and strength within the mind

Built to love, comfort and embrace and care

Built to be wise, to learn then teach

Like the yoke, in an egg, center of peace

All Around Person, All Around Friend, All Round Whatever Needed To Be

Never does what she wants to do, but always does what she has to do

Comes in different colors, shapes and sizes
Different tones of voice, types of hair and styles of clothes
Different backgrounds, educational levels and the willingness to succeed
Different but yet the same

That baby's going to a pretty little girl

And that little girls going to be a beautiful teenager

And that teenager is3 going to be a creative young lady

And that young lady is going to grow up and become an experienced woman

A woman with knowledge that have learned her limitations

And that have learned that there are no limits to limitations

All Around Person All Around Friend, All Around Whatever Needed To Be, A Woman

All Around

You Hurt Me

I should have known what we had was to good to be true
Because in too many situations we struggled in what to do

You hurt me so much I can't explain the pain
Because I wasn't like other females that tolerated the games

I would always ask you, how much did you love me?
You'll say words or numbers can't explain, neither symbols or signs

You've lied to me from day one about your past relationship
Then when I found out two years later, you lied and said you've split

All I ever wanted was for you to love me for me
Live my dreams and be happy

You're the reason why I cry myself asleep
And you're the reason why I became so afraid and weak

You're the reason why I never want to love again
And you'll be the reason why I bring my life to the end

You hurt me to the point when I think of you I cry
And to the point that there's no reason to live, just die

It's like you to took a knife and stabbed me in my heart
Because I feel like day by day I'm falling apart

And you said you love me, but you cant pick up the phone
You're selfish because you're not worried about anything that's going on

And I'm glad I'm not having a child by you
Because you're a sorry man and a sorry father too

You hurt me so
I just thought I'd express my self a little so I can grow

Only You Understand You

Face this world and all by yourself
Because I'm sure you been came to the conclusion you don't need nobody else

Happiness is within
And you're, your only friend

No one understands you and knows what's in your heart
People have forced you and the world to pull apart

Apart from life, dreams and the enjoyment, The enjoyment of what tomorrow may bring
And the fact that your happiness has been melted into other things

And that may have left you torn and maybe even alone
Maybe made you feel like you're the only one who knows what's going on

What's going on is life everyday, and it may feel like its falling apart
You even sometimes may feel like stopping the beats of your heart

I know I have, but no one will understand but me
And no one will know the hurt and pain I had to feel and see

It's your choice to walk or run
Your choice to be wise and say I've won

To be something or somebody with a good heart to share
No one will ever understand who you are, if you don't care

Where is This Going

I have so many mixed feeling boiling up inside
There's so many that I can't explain

So much I continue to hold onto
There's so much pain coming out I don't know what to do

I love, but maybe I love the wrong way
Because I continue to hear, I say things I shouldn't say

I try to be me and love from my heart
But the love I'm giving is tearing me apart

I'm sorry is not going to fix it or do anything about it
It just seems like my heart is completely split

Split in half, but not in good and bad
But more of a sad and mad

Like there's no goodness in my heart
And makes me feel like my mind, body and soul is falling apart

I love you for you but do you love me for me
Because sometimes it seems like were not happy

And at times it seems like tomorrow will be the end
And I hurt because I don't think we'll end up as friends

PAIN- WRONG TURN.. .. ..

Just Rain On Me

After the pain slowly falls the rain
The rain from the sky and the rain from your eyes

The pain that you've been holding in so long you forgot who you are
And after the rain, that's over filled, you find yourself behind bars

The pain that you been holding in because you've been hurt
The rain that made mud, because it was mixed with dirt

The dirt that's filthy and muddy, pulling you down
That mud that's covering you and want allow you to get off the ground

But stand tall and let the rain wash everything away
Then be strong and fall to your knees and pray

But instead you allow the mud to pull you in and begin to sink
Sink further and further because you're to weak to think

Think about,
 Who you are?
  Where are you going?
And most of all,
  Where you want to go?

As the rain washes everything away, stand with open arms and enjoy the rain
And know that, its okay to cry out, because after the rain I promise the sun will shine again

Why Me God?

Why did I have to be raised in a poor family?
Why did I feel like my mother abandoned me?
Why out of all the people in the world it was me crying myself to sleep at night?
Why did I have to put up so many fights?
Why was I this person that truly hated herself?
And why when I needed it the most I couldn't get help?
Why did I try to take my own life?
And why do I act without thinking twice?
Why can't I just be happy?
Why does it seem like everything only happens to me?
Why do I have a big forehead, wide hips and big lips?

Why did I wake you up this morning?
Why is it that you never missed a meal?
Why do I continue to keep a roof over your head?
Why after all you been through I'm still by your side?
Why when you fall down I help you up?
Why do I protect you from things that aren't meant to happen?
Why did I give you such talent to write?
And why did I give you such a powerful mind?
Why do I have a wonderful future laid out for you?
Why everything you've asked for I gave it to you?
And why am I the only one who has something in store for you?

Thank You

I may not say it often, but I really thank you
I thank you for helping me and being there to see me through
Through the right and wrong and the good and bad
Just being that napkin to wipe my tears when I was sad
The way you encourage me everyday to go forward and not back
And the extra effort you put in our relationship in places I slack
You're not perfect because no one is, but when it comes to me, you're as close as can be
Sometimes I ask myself why after all I said and did he still wants me
And I told myself behind that frown there's a beautiful girl that only his eyes can see
And the way I feel about you words could never say it all
I love the way no matter how hurt you may be you'll still stand tall
Tall and strong and the person that knows when some things wrong
I love the way you care and share your heart and mind with me
And most of all I love the way you love me unconditionally
You see, were going to argue and were going to fight
And I love it when you tap me on my shoulder, and we make up in the middle of the night
I love you for you and I'm willing to accept changes that'll come alone
And at the end of the day you'll always be my baby, like that Mariah song
I'm going to hold you down because that's what love is all about
And it's about:
      Making mistakes
      Learning and teaching
      Disagreeing and arguing
      Controlling and sharing
      Caring and giving
And most of all living
Living with that one you'll love forever and when we grow old all of these memories we'll share together
Thank you for loving me the way I am, forever.

Notes:

Notes:

WITH GOD ALL THINGS ARE POSSIBLE,
WITHOUT GOD NOTHING IS POSSIBLE!

www.ingramcontent.com/pod-product-compliance
Lightning Source LLC
Chambersburg PA
CBHW051718040426
42446CB00008B/942